Primary 2

ISEE

Larchmont Academics

LarchmontAcademics.com

ISBN: 9798335648158

First paperback edition.

ISEE® is a registered trademark of the Educational Records Bureau, which was not involved in the production of, and does not endorse, sponsor, or certify this product.

Published in the USA

Larchmont Academics
Los Angeles, CA

LarchmontAcademics.com

Table of Contents

Table of Contents

Preparing for the Test

What to Expect on the ISEE®

Primary 2

The ISEE® for students entering 2nd grade has three sections: auditory comprehension, reading comprehension, and mathematics. This book has practice tests for all three sections.

Section	Number of Questions	Time Allotted
Auditory Comprehension	6	7 minutes
Reading Comprehension	18	20 minutes
Break	---	5-10 minutes
Mathematics	24	26 minutes

The Sections

 ## Auditory Comprehension

In this section, you will listen to a recorded passage. You will not be able to see the passage written out. You will then answer seven questions on the content of the passage.

Top Tips:

- Start by listening to the story all the way through. Write down key names of characters to help you follow the story.

- Next, complete all of the questions for which you know the answer.

- Then, listen to the story again and listen for the answers to the questions you didn't know.

 ## Reading Comprehension

In this section, you will read three passages. Each passage will have six questions. It will usually start with a general question about the topic of the passage. There will then be more specific questions about the content.

Top Tips:

- First, read the passage quickly to get the main idea.

- Look back within the passage for the answers since they are often written in the passage. (Think of it like a scavenger hunt!)

- Answer the questions in your head before looking at the answer choices. Then pick the answer that matches best.

Mathematics

In this section, you will solve twenty-four math problems. They are mostly word problems. Common topics include addition, subtraction, data, measurement, and ordering numbers.

Top Tips:

- Write down the numbers as you see them to keep track of the key parts of the word problems.

- If you don't know how to solve a problem, guess, and return to it later.

- Recognize the keywords below to know when to add and when to subtract.

Keywords for Word Problems:

ADD +	SUBTRACT -
More	Less
All together	Difference
In All	Fewer
Increased	Gave away
Total	Left
Sum	Decrease

Timing Strategies

Practice Timing

You have about 1 minute per question. At this level, it is best to do timed practice sections and learn how that timing feels. Watching the clock too much may make you too stressed. You can also practice with smaller sections by doing 6 questions in 6 minutes. If you have any extra time, go back and check your work.

Know when to guess and move on!

When should you guess and plan to come back if you have time at the end?

-If you think it will take more than 2 minutes.

-If the content looks completely new to you.

ISEE Scoring

 The ISEE scoring process has a few steps. It starts with your **raw score** which is based on the number of questions you answered correctly. This is then converted into a **scaled score** which is accompanied by a **percentile rank**. This percentile represents how you compare to other test takers. So, if you are in the 89th percentile, this does not mean you answered 89 percent of questions correctly. Instead, it means scored higher than 89 percent of test-takers. Your percentile score is then converted into a **stanine score** with a scale marked from 1 to 9 (9 being the highest.)

Percentile ——Stanine

1-3 —— 1
4-10——2
11-22——3
23-39——4
40-59——5
60-76——6
77-88——7
89-95——8
96-99——9

Practice Test #1

Auditory Comprehension #1

6 Questions – 7 Minutes

Go to larchmontacademics.com/primary2 to listen to the passage or have a parent read the story on the next page out loud to you. You may not look at the passage while answering the questions, but you can ask them to repeat the story from the beginning.

Chop, chop, chop went the axes, cutting down spruce trees in the wintery north woods. Each year on the last day in November, Captain Herman and his crew cut trees to bring to the city in time for Christmas. The captain's wife, Hannah, and their girls, Hazel and Pearl, and little Elsie were there every year, helping. In the summer, the captain's ship was a fishing schooner, but every winter it became the *Christmas Tree Ship*. Captain Herman loaded it with trees and sailed down Lake Michigan to the city of Chicago, where everyone knew him. Hannah and the girls watched and waved goodbye on a frosty morning. Friendly gulls stayed close as the *Christmas Tree Ship* made its way down the icy waters of the winter lake.

As night fell, snowflakes fell, like stars falling all around. Night on the lake was the captain's favorite time. The quiet of the lake gave way to the hustle and bustle of the city, as the ship made its way up the Chicago River to the Clark Street Bridge. Old friends and new customers greeted the captain and asked about Hannah and their little daughters. Captain Herman had many friends. Back home in the quiet north, Hannah and Hazel, and Pearl and Elsie watched out the window for the captain's return every year. Spruce trees from far, far, away stood cheerfully decorated in cozy houses all through the city. When Captain Herman could not take trees to the city anymore, Hannah and the girls carried on the tradition for many more years.

1. What is this story mostly about?

   (A) Captain Herman chases whales.

   (B) Hannah doesn't like spruce trees.

   (C) Seagulls and snowflakes.

   (D) Captain Herman sold spruce trees to people in Chicago.

2. What is the captain's ship used for in the summer?

   (A) A pirate ship

   (B) A whaling vessel

   (C) A fishing schooner

   (D) A cruise ship

3. Who is Hannah?

   (A) The captain's daughter

   (B) The captain's wife

   (C) The captain

   (D) A ship

4. When the passage says, "The quiet of the lake gave way to the hustle and bustle of the city."
   What does "hustle and bustle" mean?

   (A) Busyness and excitement

   (B) A fierce fight

   (C) Quiet stillness

   (D) Mountains and valleys

5. When does Captain Herman start chopping each year?

   (A) After he gets home from work

   (B) The last day of November

   (C) At the beginning of the year

   (D) Before breakfast on Saturday

6. What was Captain Herman's favorite time on the ship?

    (A) When the ship was empty

    (B) When his crew sang sailing songs

    (C) When it was early morning

    (D) When it was nighttime

7. What happened when Captain Herman could not continue his tradition of taking trees to Chicago?

    (A) He gave his ship to a company to continue it.

    (B) Hannah and the girls continued it for many years.

    (C) The trees could no longer be delivered.

    (D) The ship stayed on the lake in the winter and the summer.

Reading Comprehension #1

18 Questions – 20 Minutes

Questions 1-7:

1   People had to think of ways of flying
2 if they ever hoped to get off the ground After
3 much work and study, two French brothers,
4 Jose and Jacques Montgolfier used hot air to
5 lift a balloon. They found out that hot air was
6 much lighter than cold air. They had seen how
7 smoke would always go up into the air. Soon
8 they began to lift balloons with hot air. In
9 1783, they made a very large balloon and put
10 the mouth of it over a pan of burning coal.
11 They did this to get smoke into the bag. The
12 smoke filled the bag and lifted it 18,285
13 meters into the air. It stayed in the air for ten
14 minutes and then landed a few kilometers
15 away.
16   Although this flying balloon did not
17 carry people, it was the first time that people
18 had made something that could fly. Soon after
19 this, the brothers began working with the
20 French government to build a larger and
21 better balloon that could lift 203 kilograms.
22 The first living passengers were a duck, a
23 chicken, and a sheep. They all landed safely.
24 Now it was time for two men to fly in a
25 balloon. They stayed in the air for three
26 minutes and traveled over eight kilometers.
27   Shortly after, a Frenchman, named
28 J.A. Charles, invented a balloon that used a
29 gas that is lighter than air. His gas balloon
30 went up much quicker than the hot air
31 balloons. It stayed in the air for 45 minutes
32 and landed over 24 kilometers away, on a
33 farm.

1. What is this story mostly about?

   (A) Birthday balloons

   (B) French brothers who love each other

   (C) The invention of hot air balloons

   (D) Smoke always goes up

2. In line 22, the word "passengers" means…

   (A) People who pass.

   (B) Balloon riders.

   (C) A hallway.

   (D) A paper giving permission.

3. In line 2, the phrase "get off the ground" most closely means…

   (A) Jump.

   (B) Flip.

   (C) Spin.

   (D) Fly.

4. What important fact did the French brothers discover first?

   (A) Hot air is lighter than cold air.

   (B) Animals like to ride in hot air balloons.

   (C) It is hard to get smoke into a bag.

   (D) The French government wanted to help.

5. According to the passage, why did J.A. Charles use a gas that is lighter than air?

    (A) He didn't want to copy the brothers.

    (B) It was cheaper.

    (C) To make the balloon rise faster and go farther

    (D) To win a contest

6. What is the most likely reason that the author includes lines 24-33?

    (A) To tell how hot air balloons became better

    (B) To show who won a balloon-making prize

    (C) To suggest that the reader make a hot air balloon

    (D) To teach the reader how to share work and experiments

1   The elephant's back is high and
2 arched; his body is very large and remarkably
3 round; his neck is short and thick; his ears are
4 broad; his are eyes small, but brilliant, and
5 full of expression; his legs are thick and long
6 and his feet are divided into five short, and
7 rounded toes. His nose extends into a trunk,
8 reaching to the ground, and is of more use to
9 him than our hands are to us. At the end of it
10 are nostrils through which he draws in water
11 and then he puts it in his mouth when he
12 wishes to drink. With his trunk, the elephant
13 also gathers and puts the food into his mouth,
14 selects herbs and flowers--and breathes
15 through it--so that it serves him as a nose as
16 well as hands. With it, he often throws clods
17 and stones with great force and precision.
18   On each side of his trunk, there grows
19 out of his mouth a large white tusk which is
20 ivory. These two tusks he uses, as well as his
21 trunk, to defend himself from his enemies.
22 The skin of the elephant is thick and rough,
23 resembling the bark of an old tree. A full-
24 grown elephant will weigh from eight to ten
25 thousand pounds. His color is a dark bluish-
26 brown; but some elephants are milk white.
27   The common food of the elephant
28 includes roots, leaves, and small branches of
29 trees which he pulls down with his trunk. He
30 also eats hay, oats, and almost every kind of
31 fruit. His hearing is remarkable, and he
32 delights in music. His smell is very delicate,
33 and he takes great pleasure in the scent of
34 sweet flowers and herbs. An elephant's sense
35 of touch is equally nice at the end of his trunk,
36 for he can feel the smallest thing and can even
37 pick up a piece of money or a straw from the
38 floor.

7. What is the main idea of this story?

   (A) Elephants are big.

   (B) Elephants are not alive anymore.

   (C) Elephants are amazing and interesting animals.

   (D) Elephants are often boring to watch.

8. In line 31, what does the author mean by "remarkable"?

   (A) Of no interest

   (B) Normal

   (C) Blocked

   (D) Excellent

9. According to the story in lines 18-19, what grows on either side of the elephant's trunk?

   (A) Whiskers

   (B) Tusks

   (C) Big round cheeks

   (D) Dimples

10. Why does the author say that the elephant's skin resembles "the bark of an old tree"?

    (A) Because it is thick and rough

    (B) Because it is soft and shiny

    (C) Because it is grey

    (D) Because it is thin and hairy

11. What does the writer most likely think about the elephant's senses?

    (A) They are almost useless to the animal.

    (B) They are not as good as those of other animals.

    (C) They need practice to use them well.

    (D) They are each very sensitive.

12. What is the most likely reason the author wrote this description of elephants?

    (A) To explain why elephants are not a good animal for the zoo

    (B) To show that elephants have very little brain power

    (C) To help the reader become interested in elephants

    (D) To help elephant trainers learn how to teach elephants

Questions 13 – 18:

Once upon a time in a small village, there was a curious kitten named Milo. Milo loved to explore every nook and cranny of the village. One sunny afternoon, as he was chasing a butterfly, Milo wandered far from home and got lost.

Milo found himself in a part of the village he had never seen before. The houses were different, and the streets were unfamiliar. He felt a little scared but was determined to find his way back. Soon he met a friendly dog named Max.

"Hello, little kitten," Max said kindly. "You look lost. Can I help you?"

Milo explained that he had been chasing a butterfly and lost his way. Max smiled and said, "Don't worry, I know this village well. I can help you find your way home."

Together, Milo and Max walked through the village. They passed the bakery, where the smell of fresh bread made Milo's tummy rumble. They walked by the school, where some children were playing and laughing. Finally, they reached a small park.

"Do you recognize anything here?" Max asked.

Milo looked around and saw a big oak tree with a swing. He remembered playing on that swing with his owner, Lily. "Yes, I know this place! My house is just around the corner!" he exclaimed.

Milo thanked Max for his help and hurried home. When he reached his house, Lily was standing outside, looking worried. "Milo! Where have you been? I've been so worried!" she cried as she scooped him up into her arms.

Milo purred and nuzzled Lily's cheek, happy to be home. He learned an important lesson that day: it's okay to explore, but it's always good to have a friend to help you find your way back.

13. What is this story mostly about?

    (A) The daily life of a small village and its inhabitants

    (B) A cat who got lost but returned home

    (C) The relationship between Milo and Lily

    (D) Playing safely with animals

14. In line 3, the phrase "explore every nook and cranny" means…

    (A) Knock on every door.

    (B) Clean up well.

    (C) Go into every tiny space.

    (D) See all parts of the world.

15. In line 11, the word "determined" most closely means…

    (A) Joyous.

    (B) Sad.

    (C) Afraid.

    (D) Committed.

16. Who helped Milo find his way home?

    (A) A little girl

    (B) A nice boy

    (C) A friendly dog

    (D) A butterfly

17. According to the passage, what did Milo see that reminded him where he lived?

    (A) Children playing at the school

    (B) A big bush

    (C) A big oak tree with a swing

    (D) A fancy house

18. What was Lilly's reaction when Milo returned home?

    (A) She was angry.

    (B) She was happy and relieved.

    (C) She was indifferent.

    (D) She was scared.

Mathematics #1

24 Questions – 26 Minutes

1. Three friends are at the market. They each want to be able to eat 2 apples. How many apples should they buy in total?

   (A) 2

   (B) 3

   (C) 4

   (D) 6

2. Anna is measuring a battery.

   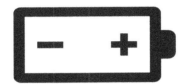

   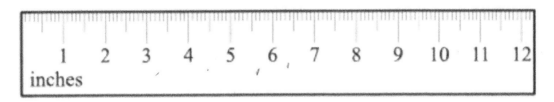

   Approximately, how long is it?

   (A) 3 inches

   (B) 4 inches

   (C) 6 inches

   (D) 7 inches

Use this chart for questions 3 and 4.

Ava counted the number of ladybugs in the garden each day.

	Monday	Tuesday	Wednesday	Thursday	Friday
5					🐞
4				🐞	🐞
3	🐞		🐞	🐞	🐞
2	🐞	🐞	🐞	🐞	🐞
1	🐞	🐞	🐞	🐞	🐞

3. On which day did she see the most ladybugs in the garden?

   (A) Monday

   (B) Tuesday

   (C) Thursday

   (D) Friday

4. On which two days did she see the same number of ladybugs in the garden?

   (A) Monday and Tuesday

   (B) Monday and Wednesday

   (C) Thursday and Friday

   (D) Tuesday and Wednesday

5. Amber and Johnny collected the number of flowers shown in the picture. They then gave 4 flowers away. Which number sentence gives the number they have left?

Amber

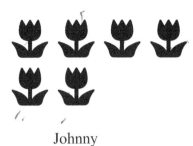

Johnny

(A) $7 + 6 - 4 = 9$

(B) $7 - 4 = 3$

(C) $7 + 6 + 4 = 17$

(D) $7 + 4 - 6 = 5$

6. Maia has 15 candies. She gives 4 to Sara and 5 to Elijah. How many candies does she have left?

(A) 5 candies

(B) 6 candies

(C) 7 candies

(D) 8 candies

7. The ball below weighs 3 pounds. The cube weighs 1 pound. Which group weighs the most?

3 pounds

1 pound

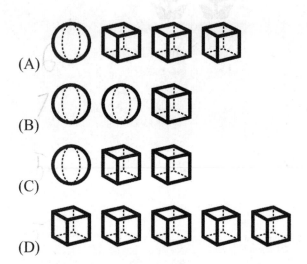

(A)

(B)

(C)

(D)

8. Emma would like to measure the width of a swimming pool. Which would be the best tool to use?

    (A) Scale

    (B) Yardstick

    (C) Thermometer

    (D) Protractor

9. How are these two shapes alike?

   (A) They both have 4 corners.

   (B) They both have 5 faces.

   (C) They both have flat bases.

   (D) They both have curved sides.

10. Ms. May's class went apple picking. Each student weighed their basket. Which shows the students' collections in order from lightest to heaviest?

Ally	Sara	Jordan	Angie
1.5 lbs	1.2 lbs	2.1 lbs	2 lbs

   (A) Sara, Ally, Angie, Jordan

   (B) Sara, Ally, Jordan, Angie

   (C) Ally, Sarah, Jordan, Angie

   (D) Jordan, Angie, Ally, Sara

11. Which group of coins would have a total value of 25 cents?

    (A) Two dimes and 1 nickel

    (B) Two dimes and 4 pennies

    (C) Twenty pennies and 5 dimes

    (D) Four nickels and 1 dime

Use this chart for questions 12 and 13.

Avery, Jorie, and Abby each sold lollipops on Friday.

Name	Number of Lollipops Sold
Avery	🍭 🍭 🍭 🍭 🍭 🍭 🍭
Jorie	🍭 🍭 🍭 🍭
Abby	🍭 🍭 🍭 🍭 🍭

12. How many more did Avery sell than Abby?

    (A) 1

    (B) 2

    (C) 4

    (D) 5

13. How many lollipops did Jorie and Abby sell combined?

    (A) 7

    (B) 8

    (C) 9

    (D) 10

14. Which is the missing piece?

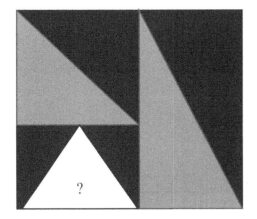

(A)

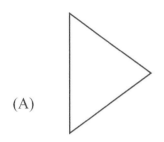

(B)

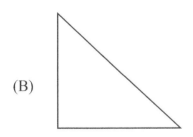

(C)

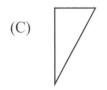

(D)

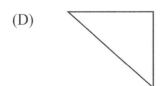

15. Jeremy wants to weigh his cat. Which tool should he use?

    (A) A scale

    (B) A ruler

    (C) A measuring cup

    (D) A beaker

16. What number is shown by the shaded squares in the picture?

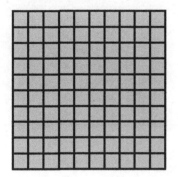 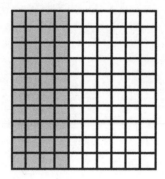 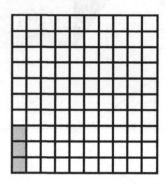

    (A) 43

    (B) 93

    (C) 134

    (D) 143

17. The graph below shows the number of books Amy sold each month.

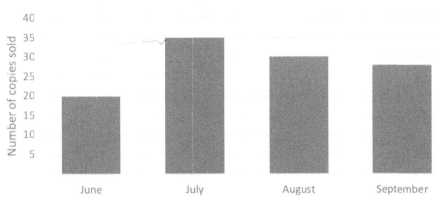

How many books did Amy sell in July?

(A) 25

(B) 30

(C) 35

(D) 40

18. What type of pattern is pictured below?

(A) AB pattern

(B) ABC pattern

(C) AAB pattern

(D) ABBA pattern

19. The word SAM looks different when flipped over the line. The word MOM looks the same.

SAM | ƧAM   MOM | MOM

Which word becomes the same when flipped over the line?

   (A) HOP

   (B) BOW

   (C) POP

   (D) WOW

20. Which shows the largest amount?

   (A) $14.53

   (B) $13.98

   (C) $14.39

   (D) $14.28

21. Henry had 14 buttons and 8 stickers to give out when he was running for class president. On Monday, he gave out 5 buttons and 3 stickers. How many of each did he have left?

   (A) 9 buttons and 5 stickers

   (B) 6 buttons and 8 stickers

   (C) 14 buttons and no stickers

   (D) 11 buttons and 3 stickers

22. What fraction of the shapes below are circles?

   (A) 1/5

   (B) 2/5

   (C) 3/5

   (D) 2

23. Which number would be next in the pattern?

4, 6, 8, 10, _?_

(A) 11

(B) 12

(C) 13

(D) 14

24. Annie had 15 eggs. She cooked 4 of the eggs. Which equation shows how many eggs she had left?

(A) $15 + 4 = 9$

(B) $15 - 9 = 6$

(C) $15 - 4 = 9$

(D) $15 - 4 = 11$

Practice Test #1 Answers

Practice Test #1 - Answers

Auditory Comprehension

1. D	4. A	7. B
2. C	5. B	
3. B	6. D	

Reading Comprehension

1. C	7. C	13. B
2. B	8. D	14. C
3. D	9. B	15. D
4. A	10. A	16. C
5. C	11. D	17. C
6. A	12. C	18. B

Mathematics

1. D	9. C	17. C
2. B	10. A	18. B
3. D	11. A	19. D
4. B	12. B	20. A
5. A	13. C	21. A
6. B	14. A	22. B
7. B	15. A	23. B
8. B	16. D	24. D

Auditory Comprehension #1

Where to Find the Answers

1. **D - Captain Herman sold spruce trees to people in Chicago.**

   4   Captain Herman and his crew cut trees to bring

   5   to the city in time for Christmas. The captain's

   20   to the hustle and bustle of the city, as the ship

   21   made its way up the Chicago River to the Clark

   22   Street Bridge. Old friends and new customers

   23   greeted the captain and asked about Hannah

2. **C - A fishing schooner**

   8   In the summer, the captain's ship was a fishing

   9   schooner, but every winter it became the

3. **B - The captain's wife**

   5   to the city in time for Christmas. The captain's

   6   wife, Hannah, and their girls, Hazel and Pearl,

4. **A - Busyness and excitement**

   19   favorite time. The quiet of the lake gave way

   20   to the hustle and bustle of the city, as the ship

   21   made its way up the Chicago River to the Clark

   22   Street Bridge. Old friends and new customers

   23   greeted the captain and asked about Hannah

   24   and their little daughters. Captain Herman had

   25   many friends. Back home in the quiet north,

5. **B - The last day of November**

   3   Each year on the last day in November,

   4   Captain Herman and his crew cut trees to bring

6. **D - When it was nighttime**

18 all around. Night on the lake was the captain's

19 favorite time. The quiet of the lake gave way

7. **B - Hannah and the girls continued it for many years.**

30 houses all through the city. When Captain

31 Herman could not take trees to the city

32 anymore, Hannah and the girls carried on the

33 tradition for many more years.

Reading Comprehension #1

Where to Find the Answers

Passage 1:

1. **C - The invention of hot air balloons**

    3   much work and study, two French brothers,

    4   Jose and Jacques Montgolfier used hot air to

    5   lift a balloon. They found out that hot air was

2. **B - Balloon riders.**

    21   better balloon that could lift 203 kilograms.

    22   The first living passengers were a duck, a

    23   chicken, and a sheep. They all landed safely.

    24   Now it was time for two men to fly in a

    25   balloon. They stayed in the air for three

3. **D - Fly.**

    1   People had to think of ways of flying

    2   if they ever hoped to get off the ground After

4. **A - Hot air is lighter than cold air.**

    5   lift a balloon. They found out that hot air was

    6   much lighter than cold air. They had seen how

    7   smoke would always go up into the air. Soon

5. **C - To make the balloon rise faster and go farther**

    27   Shortly after, a Frenchman, named

    28 J.A. Charles, invented a balloon that used a

    29 gas that is lighter than air. His gas balloon

    30 went up much quicker than the hot air

    31 balloons. It stayed in the air for 45 minutes

    32 and landed over 24 kilometers away, on a

    33 farm.

6. **A - To tell how hot air balloons became better**

    24 Now it was time for two men to fly in a

    25 balloon. They stayed in the air for three

    26 minutes and traveled over eight kilometers.

    27   Shortly after, a Frenchman, named

    28 J.A. Charles, invented a balloon that used a

    29 gas that is lighter than air. His gas balloon

    30 went up much quicker than the hot air

    31 balloons. It stayed in the air for 45 minutes

    32 and landed over 24 kilometers away, on a

    33 farm.

Passage 2:

7. **C - Elephants are amazing and interesting animals.**

    If the author writes a whole passage on the topic, they most likely think it is interesting and amazing! You could also use the process of elimination here.

8. **D – Excellent**

    31 fruit. His hearing is remarkable, and he

    32 delights in music. His smell is very delicate,

9. **B – Tusks**

18   On each side of his trunk, there grows

19 out of his mouth a large white tusk which is

10. **A - Because it is thick and rough**

22 The skin of the elephant is thick and rough,

23 resembling the bark of an old tree. A full-

11. **D - They are each very sensitive.**

4 broad; his are eyes small, but brilliant, and

5 full of expression; his legs are thick and <u>long</u>

7 rounded toes. His nose extends into a trunk,

8 reaching to the ground, and is of more use to

9 him than our hands are to us. At the end of it

31 fruit. His hearing is remarkable, and he

32 delights in music. His smell is very delicate,

33 and he takes great pleasure in the scent of

34 sweet flowers and herbs. An elephant's sense

35 of touch is equally nice at the end of his trunk,

36 for he can feel the smallest thing and can even

37 pick up a piece of money or a straw from the

38 floor.

12. **C - To help the reader become interested in elephants**

If the author writes a whole passage on the topic, they most likely think it is interesting and want to share that interest with others! You could also use the process of elimination here.

Passage 3:

13. B - A cat who got lost but returned home.

40 happy to be home. He learned an important

41 lesson that day: it's okay to explore, but it's

42 always good to have a friend to help you find

43 your way back.

14. C - Go into every tiny space

3 loved to explore every nook and cranny of the

4 village. One sunny afternoon, as he was

5 chasing a butterfly, Milo wandered far from

6 home and got lost.

7   Milo found himself in a part of the

8 village he had never seen before. The houses

9 were different, and the streets were

10 unfamiliar. He felt a little scared but was

15. D – committed

10 unfamiliar. He felt a little scared but was

11 determined to find his way back. Soon he met

16. C - A friendly dog

11 determined to find his way back. Soon he met

12 a friendly dog named Max.

13   "Hello, little kitten," Max said kindly.

14 "You look lost. Can I help you?"

15   Milo explained that he had been

16 chasing a butterfly and lost his way. Max

17 smiled and said, "Don't worry, I know this

18 village well. I can help you find your way

19 home."

17. C - A big oak tree with a swing

28   Milo looked around and saw a big oak

29 tree with a swing. He remembered playing on

30 that swing with his owner, Lily. "Yes, I know

31 this place! My house is just around the

32 corner!" he exclaimed.

18. B – She was happy and relieved.

34 hurried home. When he reached his house,

35 Lily was standing outside, looking worried.

36 "Milo! Where have you been? I've been so

37 worried!" she cried as she scooped him up

38 into her arms.

39   Milo purred and nuzzled Lily's cheek,

40 happy to be home. He learned an important

Mathematics #1

How to Solve

---

1. **D**

   Three friends are at the market. They each want to be able to eat 2 apples. How many apples should they buy in total?

   2 for each friend.

   3 friends

   $2 + 2 + 2 = 6$

2. **B**
   Anna is measuring a battery.

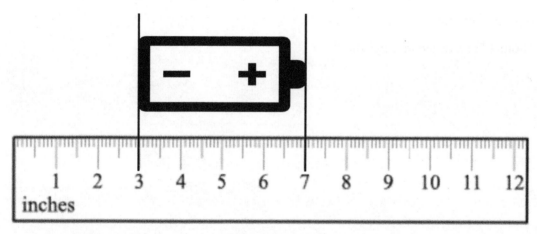

   The top of the battery is at 7 inches. The bottom of the battery is at 3 inches.

   $7 - 3 = 4$ inches

3. **D**

On which day did she see the most ladybugs in the garden?

On Friday, the line of ladybugs is the highest, so Friday is the day she saw the most.

4. **B**

On which two days did she see the same number of ladybugs in the garden?

On Monday, she saw 3 ladybugs. On Wednesday, she also saw 3 ladybugs.

5. **A**

Amber and Johnny collected the number of flowers shown in the picture. They then gave 4 flowers away. Which number sentence gives the number they have left?

Amber   Johnny

Amber has 7 flowers. Johnny has 6 flowers.

Amber plus Johnny = 7 + 6 = 13

They give 4 away, so we subtract 4.

Amber plus Johnny minus four = 7 + 6 − 4 = 9

6. **B**

Maia has 15 candies. She gives 4 to Sara and 5 to Elijah. How many candies does she have left?

Malia gives 4 to Sara → 15 − 4 = 11

She then gives 5 to Elijah → 11 − 5 = 6

7. **B**

The ball below weighs 3 pounds. The cube weighs 1 pound. Which group weighs the most?

3 pounds   1 pound

(A)
3 + 1 + 1 + 1   = 6 pounds

(B)
3 + 3 + 1   = 7 pounds

(C)
3 + 1   +   1 = 5 pounds

(D)
1 + 1 + 1 + 1 + 1 =   5 pounds

8. **B**

Emma would like to measure the width of a swimming pool. Which would be the best tool to use?

To measure the width of a pool, she needs to measure distance.

A scale measures weight, a yardstick measures distance, a thermometer measures temperature, and a protractor measures angles.

9. **C**

How are these two shapes alike?

They both have flat bases. This is the part of the shape that it rests on. They both have square flat bases that could sit flat on a table. They do not have the same number of corners or faces. Neither shape has any curved sides.

10. **A**

Ms. May's class went apple picking. Each student weighed their basket. Which shows the students' collections in order from lightest to heaviest?

Ally	Sara	Jordan	Angie
1.5 lbs	1.2 lbs	2.1 lbs	2 lbs

The lowest is Sara with 1.2 lbs, then Ally with 1.5 lbs, then Angie with 2 lbs, and the highest is Jordan with 2.1 lbs.

11. **A**

Which group of coins would have a total value of 25 cents?

(A) Two dimes and 1 nickel

$10 + 10 + 5 = 25$

(B) Two dimes and 4 pennies

$10 + 10 + 4 = 24$

(C) Twenty pennies and 5 dimes

$20 + 50 = 70$

(D) Four nickels and 1 dime

$20 + 10 = 30$

12. **B**

Avery, Jorie, and Abby each sold lollipops on Friday.

Name	Number of Lollipops Sold
Avery	🍭 🍭 🍭 🍭 🍭 🍭 🍭
Jorie	🍭 🍭 🍭 🍭
Abby	🍭 🍭 🍭 🍭 🍭

Avery sold 7 lollipops. Abby sold 5 lollipops. Avery sold 2 more than Abby.

13. **C**

How many lollipops did Jorie and Abby sell combined?

Name	Number of Lollipops Sold
Avery	🍭 🍭 🍭 🍭 🍭 🍭 🍭
Jorie	🍭 🍭 🍭 🍭
Abby	🍭 🍭 🍭 🍭 🍭

Jorie sold 4 lollipops. Abby sold 5 lollipops.

$4 + 5 = 9$

14. **A**

Which is the missing piece?

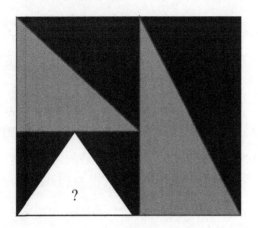

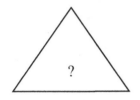 is the missing piece.

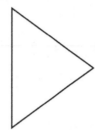 is the missing piece turned on its side.

15. **A**

Jeremy wants to weigh his cat. Which tool should he use?

Jeremy needs to measure weight. A scale measures weight, a ruler measures length, a measuring cup measures size, and a beaker measures volume.

16. **D**

What number is shown by the shaded squares in the picture?

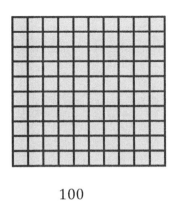 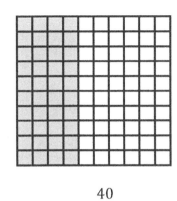 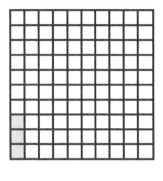

        100   40   3

100 + 40 + 3 = 143

17. **C**

The graph below shows the number of books Amy sold each month.

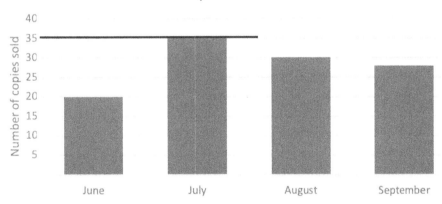

The bar for July lines up with the 35. So, she sold 35 books in July.

18. **B**

What type of pattern is pictured below?

A   B   C   A   B   C   A   B   C

Each letter represents a repeated shape. This is an ABC pattern.

19. **D**

The word SAM looks different when flipped over the line. The word MOM looks the same.

SAM | MAƧ   MOM | MOM

Which word becomes the same when flipped over the line?

For a word to be the same when flipped over the line it needs to be symmetrical and have symmetrical letters. WOW is the only option that is symmetrical with symmetrical letters.

20. **A**

Which shows the largest amount?

In order of smallest to largest: 13.98, 14.28, 14.39, 14.53

14.53 is the largest.

21. **A**

Henry had 14 buttons and 8 stickers to give out when he was running for class president. On

Monday, he gave out 5 buttons and 3 stickers. How many of each did he have left?

14 buttons – 5 buttons = 9 buttons

8 stickers – 3 stickers = 5 stickers

22. **B**

What fraction of the shapes below are circles?

2 circles and 5 shapes total

2/5

23. **B**

Which number would be next in the pattern?

4, 6, 8, 10, _?_

The pattern goes up by two.

10 + 2 = 12

24. **D**

Annie had 15 eggs. She cooked 4 of the eggs. Which equation shows how many eggs she had left?

15 eggs – 4 eggs = 11 eggs

15 – 4 = 11

Practice Test #2

Auditory Comprehension #2

6 Questions – 7 Minutes

Have a parent read the story on the next page out loud to you. You may not look at the passage while answering the questions, but you can ask them to repeat the story from the beginning.

Will you hold up my kite?" said John after unsuccessfully trying to make it fly by dragging it along the ground. Lucy kindly took it up and threw it into the air, but John forgot to start running at the same moment and the kite fell again. "Ah! It didn't work!" said the little boy.

"Try again, kids," I said. Lucy held up the kite again. This time, John ran too quickly, and the kite fell again. "Try again," I said. They tried more carefully, but a wind blew the kite into some bushes, and it got tangled.

"Not again!" cried John.

I untangled the kite and said, "Let's find a better spot and try again." We found a grassy place. I tossed the kite up, and John ran. The kite started to fly, but John stopped running. The kite fell again. "Oh John, don't stop running," I said. "Try again."

"I don't want to try anymore," John replied rather sullenly. "The kite won't fly, and I don't want to be annoyed by it anymore."

"That's silly, my little man! Are you giving up after all we have done to learn how to fly the kite? A few disappointments shouldn't discourage us. Come, I have wound up your string, Let's try again."

And he did try, and he succeeded. The kite was carried up on the breeze as lightly as a feather; and when the string was all out, John stood delighted. "Look, look, Aunt, it flies so high and pulls so hard that I can hardly hold it. I wish I had a mile of string: I am sure it would go to the end of it." After enjoying the sight for as long as he pleased, little John rolled up the string slowly. When the kite fell, he picked it up with great joy. When the kite came down, John said, "It's not broken! Can we try again tomorrow?"

"That would be fine if the weather is good. And now, tell me what you have learned today."

"I have learned to fly my kite."

"You may thank Aunt for that, John," said Lucy, "for you would have given up if she hadn't persuaded you to try again."

"Yes, children, I wish to teach you the value of perseverance, even when nothing more depends upon it than flying a kite. Whenever you fail in an attempt to do any good thing, let your motto be,—try again."

1. In this story, what are the people trying to do?

    (A) Climb a tree

    (B) Build a kite

    (C) Fly a kite

    (D) Run through the woods

2. Why did the kite fall the first time Lucy threw it?

    (A) John didn't start running.

    (B) The wind was too strong.

    (C) The kite was broken.

    (D) Lucy didn't throw it high enough.

3. Who is telling the story about Jack, Lucy, and the kite?

    (A) Their aunt

    (B) Their uncle

    (C) Their mother

    (D) Their father

4. In line 21, the sentence, " 'I don't want to try anymore,' John replied rather sullenly." What does the word "sullenly" mean?

    (A) silently

    (B) sadly

    (C) hopefully

    (D) angrily

5. Why does John say he wishes he had a mile of string?

    (A) He likes to play with strings.

    (B) He wants to measure a mile.

    (C) He wants to see the kite go higher.

    (D) He is too tired to walk a mile.

6. At the end of the story, why does Lucy say that John should thank his aunt?

    (A) She didn't let him quit trying.

    (B) She painted the kite.

    (C) She untangled the kite.

    (D) She carried the kite.

7. What did the aunt want to teach the children?

    (A) How to fly a paper airplane

    (B) How to make a cake

    (C) How to try again when they fail

    (D) How to carry their own things

Reading Comprehension #2

18 Questions – 20 Minutes

Questions 1-7:

1   Kangaroos are fascinating animals,
2 native to Australia, known for their strong
3 hind legs and unique way of moving by
4 hopping. One of the most remarkable features
5 of kangaroos is the special pouch, or
6 marsupium, on the belly of female kangaroos.
7 This pouch plays a crucial role in the life of a
8 kangaroo and its young.
9   When a baby kangaroo, called a joey,
10 is born it is extremely small and undeveloped,
11 about the size of a jellybean. Immediately
12 after birth, the tiny joey makes an incredible
13 journey from its birth canal to the mother's
14 pouch. Inside this secure and cozy pouch, the
15 joey can drink its mother's milk which is
16 necessary for it to grow and develop.
17   The pouch is not just a simple pocket;
18 it is a highly specialized structure. It has
19 strong muscles that can close the opening to
20 protect the joey from predators and harsh
21 weather. The inside of the pouch is lined with
22 fur and skin that keeps the joey warm and
23 safe.
24   As the joey grows, it begins to explore
25 the world outside the pouch, peeking out and
26 eventually venturing out for short periods.
27 However, the joey returns to the pouch for
28 nourishment and safety until it is about eight
29 months old. At this stage, the young kangaroo
30 is ready to leave the pouch permanently and
31 start living independently, though it may still
32 nurse from its mother for a while longer.
33   Kangaroos' pouches are a brilliant
34 adaptation, allowing the mother to carry and
35 nurture her young while keeping her hands
36 and forelimbs free. This unique feature
37 ensures that the joey can develop safely in a
38 protected environment until it is strong
39 enough to face the world on its own.

1. What is this story mostly about?

    (A) A kangaroo's pouch

    (B) People named Joey

    (C) Joey, the zookeeper

    (D) A kangaroo's friend

2. In line 6, what does the word "marsupium" mean?

    (A) From the planet Mars

    (B) Wonderful

    (C) A special pouch on a mother kangaroo

    (D) Warm

3. According to the story, what does a baby kangaroo drink?

    (A) Water

    (B) Plant nectar

    (C) Juice

    (D) Its mother's milk

4. Why does the author say the mother kangaroo might close her pouch?

    (A) To carry supplies for her nest

    (B) To keep her baby warm and safe

    (C) To keep herself warm

    (D) To keep extra food dry

5. What does the writer most likely think about the kangaroo's pouch?

    (A) That it is almost useless to the animal

    (B) That it is lumpy and bulky

    (C) That it is a fascinating feature of the female kangaroo

    (D) That kangaroos carry joeys in pouches for too long

6. What is the most likely reason that the author wrote this description of kangaroo pouch?

    (A) To explain this amazing feature of the kangaroo

    (B) To help other animals learn how to care for their babies

    (C) To give the reader ideas about making pouches for cats and dogs

    (D) To tell people how to rescue joeys from their mothers' pouches

1   One bright and sunny Saturday
2 morning, Malia was filled with excitement
3 because her family was going to the zoo. She
4 had always loved animals and couldn't wait to
5 see them up close. With her backpack packed
6 with snacks and a water bottle, Malia was
7 ready for an adventure.
8   As soon as they arrived at the zoo,
9 Malia grabbed a map and started planning
10 their route. "Let's visit the elephants first!"
11 she exclaimed. Malia had always been
12 fascinated by elephants. When they reached
13 the elephant enclosure, she was amazed at
14 how big they were. The zookeeper was giving
15 a talk about elephants, and Malia learned that
16 elephants use their trunks for many things,
17 like drinking water, picking up food, and even
18 giving themselves showers.
19   Next, they went to see the lions. Malia
20 watched in awe as the lions lounged under the
21 shade of a tree. The zookeeper told them that
22 lions are known as the kings of the jungle and
23 that they live in groups called prides. Malia
24 was surprised to learn that it is the lionesses
25 who do most of the hunting while the male
26 lions protect the pride.
27   After the lions, Malia and her family
28 visited the giraffes. Malia loved how tall and
29 graceful the giraffes were. She watched as
30 they used their long necks to reach the leaves
31 at the top of the trees. The zookeeper
32 explained that giraffes have long tongues that
33 help them grab leaves and that each giraffe's
34 spots are unique, just like human fingerprints.
35   As the day went on, Malia saw many
36 other animals, like zebras, kangaroos, and
37 penguins. She took lots of pictures and asked
38 the zookeepers many questions. Malia was
39 curious and wanted to learn everything she
40 could about the animals.
41   At the end of the day, Malia and her
42 family sat down for a picnic. Malia couldn't
43 stop talking about all the amazing animals she
44 had seen and the new things she had learned.
45 "Today was the best day ever," she said with a
46 big smile. "I want to come back to the zoo
47 again soon!"

7. What is this story mostly about?

   (A) Malia's trip to the zoo

   (B) Elephants, lions, and giraffes

   (C) Malia's time with family

   (D) Why zoos are important

8. In line 10, what does the author mean by "route"?

   (A) Snacks for the day

   (B) Address for the day

   (C) Path for the day

   (D) Meals and resting times for the day

9. According to the story, in lines 24-26, what is a female lion called?

   (A) A liona

   (B) A lioness

   (C) A tigress

   (D) A she-lion

10. What was the third animal that Malia and her family saw at the zoo?

   (A) The zebras

   (B) The penguins

   (C) The kangaroos

   (D) The giraffes

11. What is the most likely reason that Malia took so many photos and asked so many questions about the animals?

(A) Her parents told her she had to learn all the facts.

(B) She will soon have a test about animals at school.

(C) She was curious and excited about the zoo.

(D) She was afraid of the animals.

12. What is the most likely reason the author included lines 45-47?

(A) To show that Malia had a good time at the zoo

(B) To show that Malia didn't learn enough

(C) To help explain why Malia's parents didn't have a good time

(D) To tell Malia's parents to take her to the zoo again

Questions 13-18:

1   Our system of planets is made up of
2 the sun and everything that travels around it.
3 The sun is a star, and it is at the center of our
4 solar system. It provides light and heat to all
5 the planets. This system includes eight planets
6 and their moons, as well as asteroids, comets,
7 and other orbiting objects.
8   The eight planets in our solar system
9 are Mercury, Venus, Earth, Mars, Jupiter,
10 Saturn, Uranus, and Neptune. Mercury is the
11 closest planet to the sun. Neptune is the planet
12 farthest from the sun. Earth is the third planet
13 from the sun. These planets vary in size, with
14 some being rocky like Earth and others being
15 gaseous like Jupiter and Saturn. Each planet
16 goes around the sun in a specific path called
17 an orbit.
18   Planets have moons that orbit around
19 them. Earth, for example, has one moon, but
20 some planets have more than one moon.
21 Moons are smaller than planets and do not
22 produce any light. Instead, they reflect light
23 from the sun.
24   Asteroids and comets are smaller
25 objects that also orbit the sun. Asteroids are
26 rocky and irregularly shaped, while comets
27 are made of ice, dust, and rocky material.
28 Sometimes comets can be seen with a tail of
29 gas and dust when they come close to the sun.
30   Our solar system is a part of the Milky
31 Way galaxy. It is called that because when
32 seen from far away the group of solar systems
33 looks like a white band of light. There are
34 many other solar systems in the Milky Way
35 galaxy and many other galaxies in the
36 universe.
37   Our solar system is vast, and each
38 planet and object within it is unique.
39 Scientists study the solar system to learn more
40 about its formation and how planets and other
41 objects interact with each other.

13. What is this story mostly about?

    (A) The sun

    (B) Comets

    (C) Asteroids

    (D) Our solar system

14. In line 17, the word "orbit" means

    (A) Minty gum

    (B) Goes around

    (C) A part of a horse's bridle

    (D) A spinner

15. In the third paragraph, what important fact about moons does the author include?

    (A) They reflect the light of the sun.

    (B) They are shiny.

    (C) They produce less light than the sun.

    (D) They change size.

16. According to the passage, which planet is farthest from the sun?

    (A) Neptune

    (B) Uranus

    (C) Saturn

    (D) Jupiter

17. According to the passage, how many planets are in our solar system?

    (A) Eighty

    (B) Seven

    (C) Eight

    (D) Nine

18. What does the passage say about the Milky Way galaxy?

    (A) It is the only galaxy with solar systems.

    (B) It contains many solar systems, including ours.

    (C) It is smaller than most other galaxies.

    (D) It only has rocky planets.

Mathematics #2

1. Together, Alisa and Freddy collected the number of acorns shown in the picture.

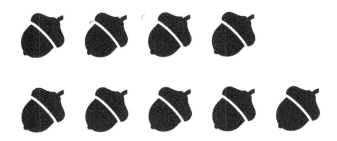

If Alisa collected 4 acorns, which number sentence shows how many acorns Freddy collected?

   (A) $9 - 4 = 5$

   (B) $9 + 4 = 13$

   (C) $4 - 5 = 13$

   (D) $9 - 3 = 6$

2. The cube below weighs 4 pounds. The cylinder weighs 2 pounds. Which group weighs the most?

      4 pounds   2 pounds

(A)

(B)

(C)

(D)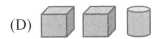

3. Josie would like to measure the distance between her house and her school. Which would be the appropriate unit?

(A) Inches

(B) Miles

(C) Pounds

(D) Liters

4. Allison has a pack of 20 chocolate candies. She wants to split them equally between herself and three other friends. How should she break them up?

(A) 4 groups of 5 chocolate candies.

(B) 4 groups of 6 chocolate candies.

(C) 3 groups of 5 chocolate candies.

(D) 5 groups of 4 chocolate candies.

5. Steven is measuring a mini fork.

Approximately how long is it?

(A) 2 inches

(B) 4 inches

(C) 5 inches

(D) 7 inches

6. Amber has 17 apples. She used 6 to make apple pie and gave 2 to her friend. How many does she have left?

    (A) 8 apples

    (B) 9 apples

    (C) 10 apples

    (D) 11 apples

7. Which shows an ABC pattern?

    (A)

    (B)

    (C)

    (D)

8. Jasmine weighed four kittens at the shelter. Which answer shows the cats in order from heaviest to lightest?

Dotty	Max	Cookie	Frankie
5.3 lbs	5.6 lbs	5.2 lbs	6.1 lbs

    (A) Frankie, Dotty, Max, Cookie

    (B) Max, Dotty, Cookie, Frankie

    (C) Frankie, Max, Dotty, Cookie

    (D) Cookie, Dotty, Max, Frankie

Use this chart for questions 9 and 10.

Charley counted the number of dogs his classmates had.

	Johnny	Dave	Brian	Jacob	Joe
4	🐕				
3	🐕			🐕	
2	🐕			🐕	
1	🐕	🐕		🐕	🐕

9. Which friend does not have a dog?

   (A) Johnny

   (B) Dave

   (C) Brian

   (D) Jacob

10. How many more dogs does Jacob have than Dave?

   (A) 1

   (B) 2

   (C) 3

   (D) 4

78

11. How are these two shapes alike?

   (A) They both have eight corners.

   (B) They both have curved sides.

   (C) They both have 6 edges.

   (D) They both are the same size.

12. Which group of coins would have a total value of 16 cents?

   (A) One quarter and one penny

   (B) One dime and one nickel

   (C) Three nickels and a penny

   (D) Ten pennies and a dime

13. Which is the missing piece?

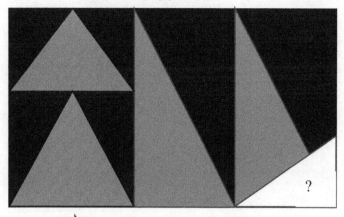

(A)

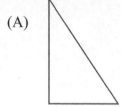

(B)

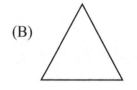

(C)

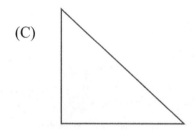

(D)

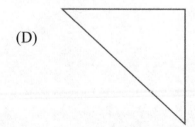

80

Use the chart below for questions 14 and 15.

The chart shows how many dumplings each of the three friends made.

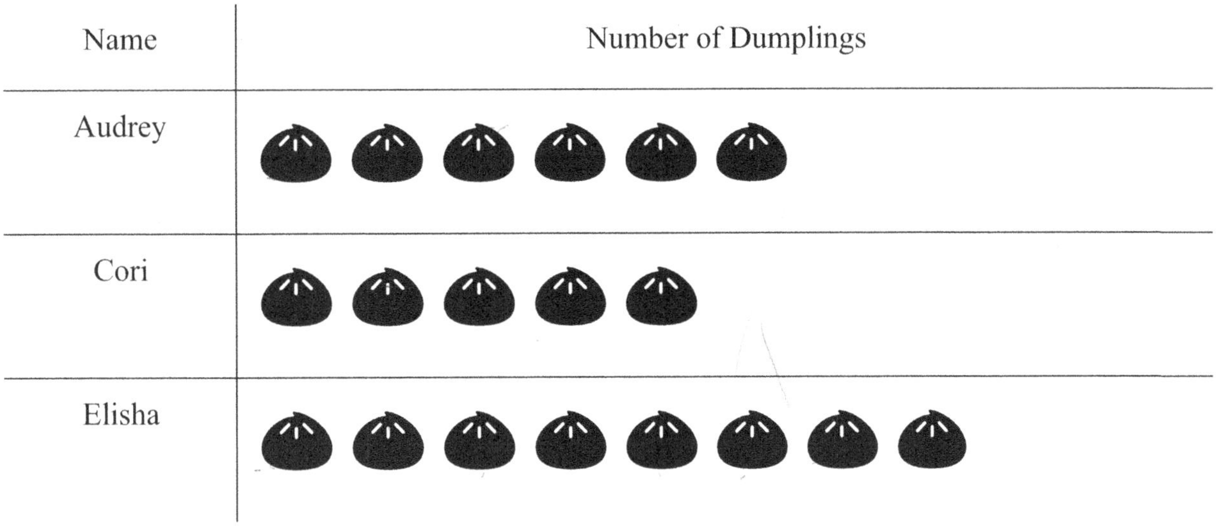

Name	Number of Dumplings
Audrey	🥟🥟🥟🥟🥟🥟
Cori	🥟🥟🥟🥟🥟
Elisha	🥟🥟🥟🥟🥟🥟🥟🥟

14. How many dumplings did the three friends make altogether?

    (A) 8

    (B) 11

    (C) 19

    (D) 20

15. How many more dumplings did Elisha make than Audrey?

    (A) 1

    (B) 2

    (C) 3

    (D) 4

16. Which shows the largest amount?

   (A) $9.48

   (B) $8.92

   (C) $9.69

   (D) $9.81

17. Addison had 17 muffins. She gave 4 to Sara and ate 3. Which number sentence shows how many she had left?

   (A) 17 – 4 – 3 = 10

   (B) 17 – 10 = 7

   (C) 17 – 3 = 14

   (D) 17 – 4 = 13

18. What number is shown by the shaded squares in the picture?

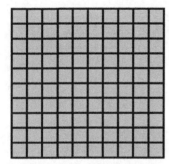 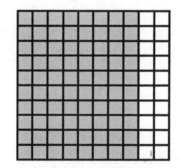 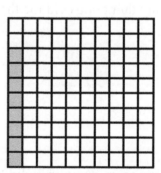

   (A) 189

   (B) 188

   (C) 178

   (D) 88

19. What fraction of the pie is shaded?

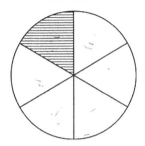

(A) 1/5

(B) 2/5

(C) 1/6

(D) 1/7

20. What is the missing number in the pattern?

5, 8, 11, _?_, 17

(A) 3

(B) 12

(C) 13

(D) 14

21. Which of the following shapes is symmetrical across a horizontal line?

(A)

(B)

(C)

(D)

22. Emmy had a pack of 12 donuts. She sold 4 donuts. Sarah gave her 6 more donuts. How many donuts does Emmy have now?

   (A) 6

   (B) 8

   (C) 12

   (D) 14

23. For 5 days, Kevin tracked how many birds he saw each day.

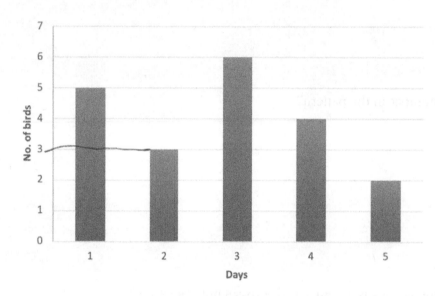

   How many birds did he see on the second day?

   (A) 2

   (B) 3

   (C) 4

   (D) 5

24. How many sides does an octagon have?

   (A) 5

   (B) 6

   (C) 7

   (D) 8

Practice Test #2 Answers

Practice Test #2 - Answers

Auditory Comprehension

1. C	4. B	7. C
2. A	5. C	
3. A	6. A	

Reading Comprehension

1. A	7. A	13. D
2. C	8. C	14. B
3. D	9. B	15. A
4. B	10. D	16. A
5. C	11. C	17. C
6. A	12. A	18. B

Mathematics

1. A	9. C	17. A
2. D	10. B	18. B
3. B	11. A	19. C
4. A	12. C	20. D
5. C	13. A	21. B
6. B	14. C	22. D
7. A	15. B	23. B
8. C	16. D	24. D

Auditory Comprehension #2

Where to Find the Answers

1. **C - Fly a kite**

   1   Will you hold up my kite?" said John after

   2   unsuccessfully trying to make it fly by

   3   dragging it along the ground. Lucy kindly

   4   took it up and threw it into the air, but John

2. **A - John didn't start running.**

   4   took it up and threw it into the air, but John

   5   forgot to start running at the same moment

   6   and the kite fell again. "Ah! It didn't work!"

3. **A - Their aunt**

   32   John stood delighted. "Look, look, Aunt, it

   33   flies so high and pulls so hard that I can

   45   "You may thank Aunt for that, John," said

   46   Lucy, "for you would have given up if she

   47   hadn't persuaded you to try again."

4. **B – Sadly**

   18   The kite fell again. "Oh John, don't stop

   19   running," I said. "Try again."

   20   "I don't want to try anymore," John

   21   replied rather sullenly. "The kite won't fly,

   22   and I don't want to be annoyed by it

   23   anymore."

5. **C – He wants to see the kite go higher.**

30 kite was carried up on the breeze as lightly as

31 a feather; and when the string was all out,

32 John stood delighted. "Look, look, Aunt, it

33 flies so high and pulls so hard that I can

34 hardly hold it. I wish I had a mile of string: I

35 am sure it would go to the end of it." After

6. **A - She didn't let him quit trying.**

8   "Try again, kids," I said. Lucy held up the

9 kite again. This time, John ran too quickly,

10 and the kite fell again. "Try again," I said.

14   I untangled the kite and said, "Let's find a

15 better spot and try again." We found a grassy

24   "That's silly, my little man! Are you

25 giving up after all we have done to learn how

26 to fly the kite? A few disappointments

27 shouldn't discourage us. Come, I have wound

28 up your string, Let's try again."

7. **C - How to try again when they fail**

48   "Yes, children, I wish to teach you the

49 value of perseverance, even when nothing

50 more depends upon it than flying a kite.

51 Whenever you fail in an attempt to do any

52 good thing, let your motto be,—try again."

Reading Comprehension #2

Where to Find the Answers

Passage 1:

1. **A -A kangaroo's pouch**

    4 hopping. One of the most remarkable features

    5 of kangaroos is the special pouch, or

    6 marsupium, on the belly of female kangaroos.

    7 This pouch plays a crucial role in the life of a

    8 kangaroo and its young.

    14 pouch. Inside this secure and cozy pouch, the

    15 joey can drink its mother's milk which is

    16 necessary for it to grow and develop.

    17   The pouch is not just a simple pocket;

    18 it is a highly specialized structure. It has

    19 strong muscles that can close the opening to

    20 protect the joey from predators and harsh

    21 weather. The inside of the pouch is lined with

    22 fur and skin that keeps the joey warm and

    23 safe.

    33   Kangaroos' pouches are a brilliant

    34 adaptation, allowing the mother to carry and

    35 nurture her young while keeping her hands

    36 and forelimbs free. This unique feature

    37 ensures that the joey can develop safely in a

    38 protected environment until it is strong

    39 enough to face the world on its own.

2. **C - A special pouch on a mother kangaroo**

    4 hopping. One of the most remarkable features

    5 of kangaroos is the special pouch, or

    6 marsupium, on the belly of female kangaroos.

3. **D - Its mother's milk**

    14 pouch. Inside this secure and cozy pouch, the

    15 joey can drink its mother's milk which is

    16 necessary <u>for it</u> to grow and develop.

4. **B - To keep her baby warm and safe**

    18 it is a highly specialized structure. It has

    19 strong muscles that can close the opening to

    20 protect the joey from predators and harsh

    21 weather. The inside of the pouch is lined with

    22 fur and skin that keeps the joey warm and

    23 safe.

5. **C - That it is a fascinating feature of the female kangaroo**

    4 hopping. One of the most remarkable features

    5 of kangaroos is the special pouch, or

    6 marsupium, on the belly of female kangaroos.

    33   Kangaroos' pouches are a brilliant

    34 adaptation, allowing the mother to carry and

    35 nurture her young while keeping her hands

    36 and forelimbs free. This unique feature

6. **A - To explain this amazing feature of the kangaroo**

   If the author writes a whole passage on the topic, they

   most likely think it is amazing and want to share that

   interest with others! You could also use the process of

   elimination here.

Passage 2:

7. **A - Malia's trip to the zoo**

  2   morning, Malia was filled with excitement

  3   because her family was going to the zoo. She

  8   As soon as they arrived at the zoo,

  9   Malia grabbed a map and started planning

37   penguins. She took lots of pictures and asked

38   the zookeepers many questions. Malia was

46   big smile. "I want to come back to the zoo

47   again soon!"

8. **C - Path for the day**

  8   As soon as they arrived at the zoo,

  9   Malia grabbed a map and started planning

10   their route. "Let's visit the elephants first!"

9. **B – A lioness**

24   was surprised to learn that it is the lionesses

25   who do most of the hunting while the male

26   lions protect the pride.

10. **D – The giraffes**

10   their route. "Let's visit the elephants first!"

19   Next, they went to see the lions. Malia

27   After the lions, Malia and her family

28   visited the giraffes. Malia loved how tall and

11. C - She was curious and excited about the zoo.

2 morning, Malia was filled with excitement

3 because her family was going to the zoo. She

4 had always loved animals and couldn't wait to

5 see them up close. With her backpack packed

38 the zookeepers many questions. Malia was

39 curious and wanted to learn everything she

40 could about the animals.

12. A - To show that Malia had a good time at the zoo

42 family sat down for a picnic. Malia couldn't

43 stop talking about all the amazing animals she

44 had seen and the new things she had learned.

45 "Today was the best day ever," she said with a

46 big smile. "I want to come back to the zoo

47 again soon!"

Passage 3:

13. **D - Our solar system**

1   Our system of planets is made up of

2 the sun and everything that travels around it.

3 The sun is a star, and it is at the center of our

4 solar system. It provides light and heat to all

5 the planets. This system includes eight planets

6 and their moons, as well as asteroids, comets,

7 and other orbiting objects.

8   The eight planets in our solar system

9 are Mercury, Venus, Earth, Mars, Jupiter,

10 Saturn, Uranus, and Neptune. Mercury is the

30   Our solar system is a part of the Milky

31 Way galaxy. It is called that because when

37   Our solar system is vast, and each

38 planet and object within it is unique.

39 Scientists study the solar system to learn more

14. **B - Goes around**

15 gaseous like Jupiter and Saturn. Each planet

16 goes around the sun in a specific path called

17 an orbit.

18   Planets have <u>moons</u> that orbit around

15. **A - They reflect the light of the sun.**

21 Moons are smaller than planets and do not

22 produce any light. Instead, they reflect light

23 from the sun.

16. A – Neptune

11 closest planet to the sun. Neptune is the planet

12 farthest from the sun. Earth is the third planet

17. C – Eight

8   The eight planets in our solar system

18. B - It contains many solar systems, including ours.

30   Our solar system is a part of the Milky

31 Way galaxy. It is called that because when

32 seen from far away the group of solar systems

33 looks like a white band of light. There are

34 many other solar systems in the Milky Way

35 galaxy and many other galaxies in the

36 universe.

Mathematics #2– How to Solve

1. **A**

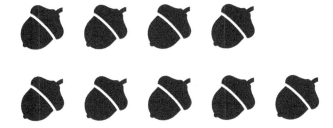

If Alisa collected 4 acorns, which number sentence shows how many acorns Freddy collected?

9 acorns are pictured. Alisa collected 4.

9 – 4 = the number of acorns Freddy collected.

9 – 4 = 5

2. **D**

The cube below weighs 4 pounds. The cylinder weighs 2 pounds. Which group weighs the most?

(A)

4 + 2 = 6

(B)

2 + 2 + 2 + 2 = 8

(C)

4 + 4 = 8

(D)

4 + 4 + 2 = 10

3. **B**

   Josie would like to measure the distance between her house and her school. Which would be the appropriate unit?

   She needs to measure a distance. Inches measure lengths, miles measure distance, pounds measure weight, and liters measure volume.

4. **A**

   Allison has a pack of 20 M&Ms. She wants to split them equally between herself and three other friends. How should she break them up?

   Allison + 3 other friends = 4 friends total so she needs 4 groups.

   Test A and B:

   (A) 4 groups of 5 M&Ms → 5 + 5 + 5 + 5 = 20

   (B) 4 groups of 6 M&Ms → 4 + 4 + 4 + 4 + 4 = 26

5. **C**

   Starts at 2 inches and ends at 7 inches.

   7 − 2 = 5 inches

6. **B**

Amber has 17 apples. She used 6 to make apple pie and gave 2 to her friend. How many does she have left?

$17 - 6 = 11$

$11 - 2 = 9$

7. **A**

Which shows an ABC pattern?

(A)
A   B   C   A   B   C

(B)
A   A   B   C   C

(C)
A   B   A   B   A   B

(D)
B   C   A   C   B

8. **C**

   Jasmine weighed four kittens at the shelter. Which shows the cats in order from heaviest to lightest?

Dotty	Max	Cookie	Frankie
5.3 lbs	5.6 lbs	5.2 lbs	6.1 lbs

   Frankie is 6.1 lbs which is the heaviest. Max is next at 5.6 lbs. Cookie is 5.3 lbs. Dotty is the lightest at 5.2 lbs.

   Frankie, Max, Cookie, then Dotty.

Use this chart for questions 9 and 10.

Charley counted the number of dogs his classmates had.

9. **C**

   Which friend does not have a dog?

   Brian has no dogs above his name. So, he does not have a dog.

10. **B**

   How many more dogs does Jacob have than Dave?

   Jacob has 3 dogs. Dave has 1 dog. Jacob has 2 more dogs than Dave.

98

11. **A**

How are these two shapes alike?

They both have eight corners. They do not have curved sides, they have more than six edges, and we can't tell the size.

12. **C**

Which group of coins would have a total value of 16 cents?

(A) One quarter and one penny → 25 + 1 = 26 cents

(B) One dime and one nickel → 10 + 5 = 15 cents

(C) Three nickels and a penny → 15 + 1 = 16 cents

(D) Ten pennies and a dime → 10 + 10 = 20 cents

13. **A**

Which is the missing piece?

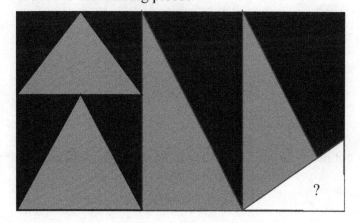

Missing piece:

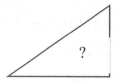

Option A is the same but rotated:

Use the chart below for questions 14 and 15.

The chart shows how many dumplings each of the three friends made.

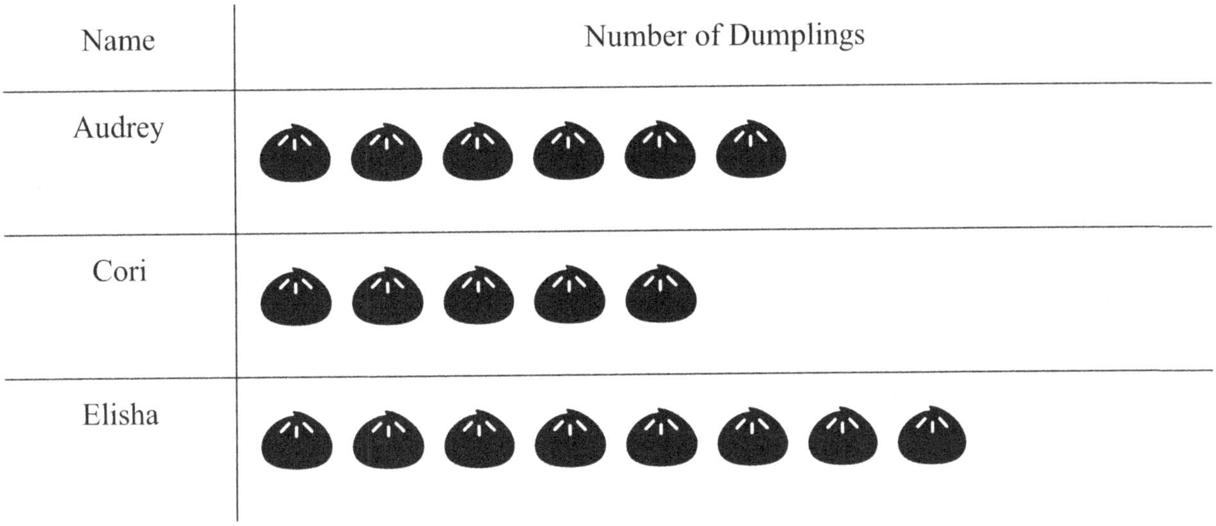

Name	Number of Dumplings
Audrey	🥟 🥟 🥟 🥟 🥟 🥟
Cori	🥟 🥟 🥟 🥟 🥟
Elisha	🥟 🥟 🥟 🥟 🥟 🥟 🥟 🥟

14. **C**

How many dumplings did the three friends make altogether?

Audrey made 6.

Cori made 5.

Elisha made 8.

$6 + 5 + 8 = 19$

15. **B**

How many more dumplings did Elisha make than Audrey?

Elisha made 8 and Audrey made 6.

$8 - 6 = 2$

16. **D**

Which shows the largest amount?

(A) $9.48

(B) $8.92

(C) $9.69

(D) $9.81

First, look for the highest number in the ones place. This is 9 so we can cross out B. Next, look for the highest number after the decimal (the tenths place). This is 8. So, 9.81 is the highest number.

17. **A**

Addison had 17 muffins. She gave 4 to Sara and ate 3. Which number sentence shows how many she had left?

17 muffins – 4 muffins for Sara – 3 muffins she ate.

17 – 4 – 3 = 10

18. **B**

What number is shown by the shaded squares in the picture?

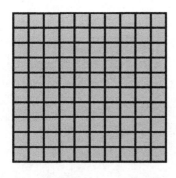   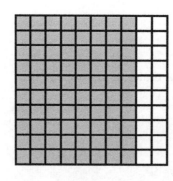   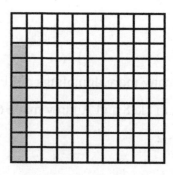

100   80   8

100 + 80 + 8 = 188

19. **C**

What fraction of the pie is shaded?

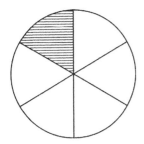

     1 part is shaded.

     6 parts total.

     1/6

20. **D**

What is the missing number in the pattern?

5, 8, 11, _?_, 17

The numbers go up by 3 in the pattern (5 + 3 = 8 and 8 + 3 = 11)

11 + 3 = 14

21. **B**

Which of the following shapes is symmetrical across a horizontal line?

This means that if you fold it over the line that is drawn in, both sides will match up. B is the only one that works.

(A)

(B)

(C)

(D)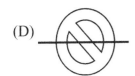

22. **D**

Emmy had a pack of 12 donuts. She sold 4 donuts. Sarah gave her 6 more donuts. How many donuts does Emmy have now?

She starts with 12 donuts and sells 4 → 12 − 4 = 8

Sarah then gives her 6 more donuts → 8 + 6 = 14

23. **B**

For 5 days, Kevin tracked how many birds he saw each day.

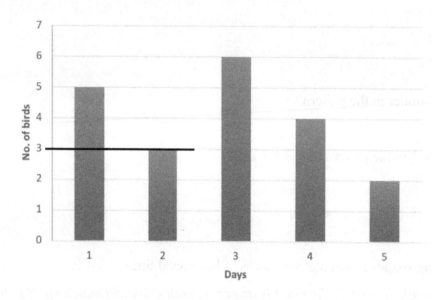

How many birds did he see on the second day?

The bar above day 2 goes up to the 3. So, he saw 3 birds.

24. **D**

How many sides does an octagon have?

"Octa" means 8, so an octagon has 8 sides.

Practice Test #3

Auditory Comprehension

6 Questions – 7 Minutes

Have a parent read the story on the next page out loud to you. You may not look at the passage while answering the questions, but you can ask them to repeat the story from the beginning.

The lion is often called the "king of beasts." He is a big and powerful animal, standing three to four feet tall and measuring six to nine feet long. His coat is yellowish-brown, and he has a great, shaggy mane around his neck that makes him look majestic. Lions live in the forests of Asia and Africa, where they are feared by both people and animals. However, if a lion is taken when young, it can be tamed and might even show kindness to its keeper.

In a zoo in Brussels, there was a large lion named Danco. One day, Danco's cage needed repairs. The keeper, William, asked a repairman to fix it, but the repairman was too scared to go near the lion alone. So, William went into the cage and led Danco to the upper part of it while the repairs were made.

William played with the lion for a while, and then both he and Danco fell asleep. The repairman finished his work and called out for William to come and see it, but William didn't answer. The repairman got worried that the lion had hurt William, so he crept around the outside of the cage. To his surprise, he saw the lion and William sleeping side by side contently like two brothers. The repairman was so astonished that he yelped.

The lion woke up and stared at the repairman with an angry look. He placed his paw on William's chest as if to say, "Don't touch him." Then the lion lay down to sleep again. The repairman was worried that William was hurt. He ran out and told other people what he had seen. Some people came and opened the cage door. They tried to wake William, who rubbed his eyes, looked around, and said he was happy with his nap. He shook the lion's paw kindly and then left the cage unharmed.

1. What is this story mostly about?

   (A) The strength and majesty of lions in the wild

   (B) The relationship between a lion and his keeper

   (C) The history of a lion named William

   (D) The job of a repairman at a zoo

2. Why is the lion called the "king of beasts"?

   (A) Because he has a sparkly crown

   (B) Because he is very strong and looks majestic

   (C) Because he lives in a palace

   (D) Because he is louder than the other animals

3. In the story, what is the Lion's name?

   (A) William

   (B) Davey

   (C) Brussels

   (D) Danco

4. Why was the repairman afraid to fix the lion's cage alone?

   (A) He thought the lion might escape.

   (B) He thought the lion might hurt him.

   (C) He didn't have the right tools.

   (D) He was too tired.

5. What did William do to help the repairman fix the lion's cage?

   (A) He asked the lion to leave.

   (B) He tied up the lion.

   (C) He led the lion to the upper part of the cage.

   (D) He put the lion on a chain.

6. What does the writer mean by "contently" when the says they slept "contently like two brothers?"

   (A) comfortably and happily

   (B) restlessly

   (C) crowdedly

   (D) fearfully

7. Why does the author include the part about the zookeeper shaking the lion's paw at the end of the story?

   (A) To report a list of the lion's tricks

   (B) To show that lions at the zoo are never dangerous

   (C) To prove that the zookeeper was friendly with the lion

   (D) To make the reader afraid of lions

Reading Comprehension #3

18 Questions – 20 Minutes

Questions 1-6:

1   Bees are small insects, but they are
2   very important to our world. Bees help plants
3   grow by carrying pollen from one flower to
4   another. This process is called pollination.
5   Without bees, many plants would not be able
6   to produce fruits and seeds.
7   Bees live in large groups called
8   colonies. Each colony has one queen bee,
9   many worker bees, and a few drones. The
10 queen bee's job is to lay eggs. Worker bees do
11 all the other jobs, like finding food, building
12 the hive, and taking care of the young bees.
13 Drones have one job, and that is to mate with
14 the queen.
15   Bees make their homes in hives. A
16 hive can be found in a tree, a wall, or even in
17 a beekeeper's box. Inside the hive, bees build
18 honeycombs out of wax. The honeycombs
19 have many small cells where bees store honey
20 and pollen and raise their young.

21   Bees communicate with each other
22 through a special dance. When a worker bee
23 finds a good source of food, it returns to the
24 hive and performs a dance. This dance tells
25 the other bees where the food is located.
26   Honeybees produce honey as food for
27 their young and as a way of storing food.
28 Honey is sweet and delicious. People have
29 been collecting honey from bees for
30 thousands of years. Honey can be used in
31 many different ways, like sweetening tea or
32 baking cakes.
33   Even though bees can sting, they
34 usually only do this when they feel
35 threatened. It is important to be calm and
36 gentle around bees, so they do not feel the
37 need to sting.
38   Bees are amazing creatures that do a
39 lot for our environment. It is important to
40 protect bees so they can continue to help our
41 plants grow and provide us with honey.

1. What is this story mostly about?

   (A) How bees build their hives

   (B) The different jobs on a bee farm

   (C) The importance of bees and why they are interesting

   (D) The way bees protect themselves

2. What is a bee colony composed of?

   (A) One queen bee, many worker bees, and a few drones

   (B) Many queens, a few workers, and one drone

   (C) Only worker bees

   (D) Many queens and drones

3. What do worker bees do in the colony?

   (A) Lay eggs

   (B) Eat honey

   (C) Find food, build the hive, and take care of young bees

   (D) Sting other insects

4. In line 18, what does the word "cells" mean?

   (A) Phones

   (B) Jails

   (C) Sections

   (D) Jars

5. What is the reason the author gives for why a worker bee performs a dance?

   (A) To entertain the queen

   (B) To teach other bees the correct moves

   (C) To communicate where food is located

   (D) To get exercise

6. What does the author most likely think about bees?

   (A) They are dangerous and should be avoided.

   (B) They are fascinating and important to our environment.

   (C) They are only useful for making honey.

   (D) They are annoying because they can sting.

1   Planting a garden can be a fun and
2 rewarding activity. Gardens can be small or
3 large, and you can grow many different kinds
4 of plants. Whether you want to grow flowers,
5 vegetables, or herbs, there are a few steps you
6 need to follow to get started.

7   First, you need to choose a good spot
8 for your garden. Plants need sunlight to grow,
9 so pick a place that gets plenty of sun. Make
10 sure the soil is good for planting. You might
11 need to add compost or fertilizer to help your
12 plants grow strong and healthy.

13   Next, decide what you want to plant.
14 If you are growing vegetables, you might
15 choose tomatoes, carrots, or lettuce. For a
16 flower garden, you could plant roses,
17 sunflowers, or daisies. Herbs like basil, mint,
18 and parsley are also good choices.

19   Once you have chosen your plants, it
20 is time to start planting. Dig small holes in the
21 soil for your seeds or plants. Make sure to
22 space them out so they have room to grow.

23 Cover the seeds with soil and gently pat it
24 down. If you are planting small plants, make
25 sure their roots are covered with soil.

26   After planting, water your garden
27 well. Plants need water to grow, so keep the
28 soil moist but not too wet. It is important to
29 water your garden regularly, especially if it
30 does not rain.

31   As your garden grows, you will need
32 to take care of it. Pull out any weeds that
33 might grow around your plants. Weeds can
34 take nutrients and water away from your
35 plants. Also, watch out for insects that might
36 harm your garden. You can use natural
37 methods to keep pests away, like planting
38 marigolds that repel bugs.

39   Planting a garden can teach you a lot
40 about nature and help you enjoy the outdoors.
41 You will be proud of the beautiful flowers or
42 delicious vegetables you grow. Plus,
43 gardening is a great way to spend time with
44 family and friends. Happy gardening!

7. What is this story mostly about?

   (A) The different types of plants you can grow in a garden

   (B) The steps and tips for planting and taking care of a garden

   (C) The best places to plant a garden

   (D) How to keep insects away from your garden

8. In line 2, the phrase "rewarding activity" most closely means…

   (A) An enjoyable way to spend time.

   (B) A prize for doing chores.

   (C) A way to make money.

   (D) An expensive trip.

9. According to the story, what is the second step when planting a garden?

   (A) Choose a spot.

   (B) Harvest the vegetables.

   (C) Choose what to plant.

   (D) Start planting seeds or small plants.

10. Why does the author say you should space out the plants?

   (A) To help the insects collect pollen

   (B) To keep vegetables and flowers separate

   (C) To make a pretty pattern

   (D) To give them space to grow

11. Why is it important to pull out weeds from your garden?

   (A) They make the garden look messy.

   (B) They can take nutrients and water away from your plants.

   (C) They attract insects.

   (D) To give you exercise.

12. What does the author think about gardening?

   (A) It makes the environment less natural.

   (B) It is difficult and can be dangerous.

   (C) It is a good way to make money.

   (D) It is a great way to enjoy nature.

1   Have you ever seen a butterfly?
2   Butterflies are beautiful creatures with
3   colorful wings. But did you know that
4   butterflies do not start their lives as
5   butterflies? They go through a special process
6   called metamorphosis.

7   A butterfly's life begins as an egg. The
8   butterfly lays her eggs on the leaves of plants.
9   After a few days, a tiny caterpillar hatches
10 from the egg. The caterpillar is very hungry
11 and starts to eat the leaves around it. As it
12 eats, the caterpillar grows bigger and bigger.
13 It even sheds its skin several times because it
14 gets too tight.

15 Once the caterpillar is fully grown, it
16 stops eating and finds a safe place to rest. It
17 forms a hard shell around itself called a
18 chrysalis. Inside the chrysalis, the caterpillar's
19 body changes completely. This transformation
20 is amazing and takes about two weeks.

21 Finally, the chrysalis opens, and a
22 butterfly emerges. At first, the butterfly's
23 wings are wet and crumpled. The butterfly
24 must wait for its wings to dry before it can
25 fly. When the wings are ready, the butterfly
26 flies away to find flowers. It drinks nectar
27 from the flowers using a long, tube-like
28 tongue, called a proboscis.

29 Butterflies are not just pretty to look
30 at; they are also important for the
31 environment. As butterflies move from flower
32 to flower, they help plants by spreading
33 pollen. This helps plants grow and produce
34 fruits and seeds.

35 The life cycle of a butterfly is a
36 wonderful example of nature's magic. From a
37 tiny egg to a beautiful butterfly, the journey is
38 full of changes and surprises. The next time
39 you see a butterfly, you will know all about
40 its incredible transformation.

13. What is this story mostly about?

    (A) The different types of butterflies

    (B) The life cycle and transformation of a butterfly

    (C) How to catch a butterfly

    (D) The best plants for caterpillars

14. What does a caterpillar do after it hatches from the egg?

    (A) Flies away

    (B) Starts eating leaves

    (C) Builds a nest

    (D) Lays eggs

15. According to the passage, how long does the butterfly's transformation take?

    (A) Three weeks

    (B) Two days

    (C) Two weeks

    (D) One month

16. What is a chrysalis?

    (A) A type of butterfly

    (B) A hard shell around the caterpillar

    (C) A flower that butterflies like

    (D) The wings of a butterfly

17. In line 36, the phrase "nature's magic" most closely refers to…

    (A) How a caterpillar changes into a butterfly.

    (B) How people make potions.

    (C) How people build with items from nature.

    (D) How fog makes everything disappear.

18. In lines 29-34, why does the writer most likely say butterflies are good for the environment?

    (A) They make the world more beautiful.

    (B) They spread pollen.

    (C) They show people how to change.

    (D) They make the air cooler.

Mathematics #3

1. Cameron is measuring her cupcake.

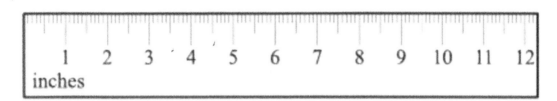

   Approximately, how wide is it?

   (A) 2 inches

   (B) 3 inches

   (C) 5 inches

   (D) 7 inches

2. Which shows the smallest amount?

   (A) $4.34

   (B) $4.81

   (C) $5.01

   (D) $4.90

Use this chart for questions 3 and 4.

Steven counted the number of eggs in his chicken coop each day.

	Monday	Tuesday	Wednesday	Thursday	Friday
4					🥚
3			🥚		🥚
2		🥚	🥚	🥚	🥚
1	🥚	🥚	🥚	🥚	🥚

3. On which two days did he see the same number of eggs?

   (A) Monday and Tuesday

   (B) Tuesday and Wednesday

   (C) Tuesday and Thursday

   (D) Wednesday and Friday

4. On which day did he count three eggs in the coop?

    (A) Monday

    (B) Wednesday

    (C) Thursday

    (D) Friday

5. Stephanie wants to make 3 bracelets for each of her 4 friends. How many bracelets should she make in total?

    (A) 3

    (B) 7

    (C) 10

    (D) 12

6. Alvin has 24 stuffed animals. He donated 12 stuffed animals. He then got two more for his birthday. How many does he have now?

    (A) 10

    (B) 12

    (C) 14

    (D) 36

7. Which shows an AB pattern?

    (A)

    (B)

    (C)

    (D)

8. Ms. Anita's class collected bags of leaves.

Sam	Mary	Asher	Judah
16.4 oz	15.4 oz	16.8 oz	15.9 oz

Who collected the most?

(A) Sam

(B) Mary

(C) Asher

(D) Judah

9. What fraction does the shaded part represent?

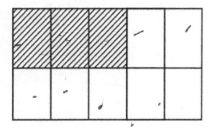

(A) 3/7

(B) 3/8

(C) 3/10

(D) 3

10. What is the missing number in the pattern?

3, 6, 12, _?__

(A) 15

(B) 18

(C) 20

(D) 24

11. What number is shown by the shaded squares in the picture?

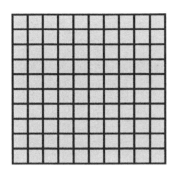 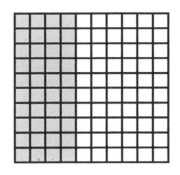 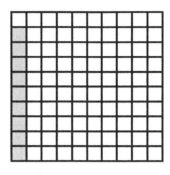

(A) 149

(B) 188

(C) 139

(D) 99

12. Which of the following shapes is symmetrical across a vertical line?

(A)

(B)

(C)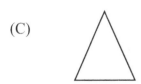

(D)

13. How are these two shapes alike?

(A) They are both squares.

(B) They are both rectangles.

(C) They both have six edges.

(D) They are both the same size.

14. Kayla has 22 stickers. She gave 6 to Sara and 4 to Sally. Which number sentence shows how many she had left?

(A) $22 - 6 + 4 = 20$

(B) $22 - 6 - 4 = 12$

(C) $22 - 6 = 20 - 4$

(D) $22 - 8 = 14$

15. Jaelyn has 15 buttons. She wants to split them equally between herself and two other friends. How many should each person get?

(A) 3

(B) 5

(C) 6

(D) 7

16. Emerson would like to measure flour for cookies. Which is the appropriate unit?

(A) Inches

(B) Pounds

(C) Cups

(D) Meters

17. Which of the following would have the value of 23 cents?

   (A) One quarter and three pennies

   (B) One dime, one nickel, and three pennies

   (C) Two dimes and three pennies

   (D) Two nickels and three pennies

Use the chart below for questions 18 and 19.

The chart shows how many apples three friends picked.

Name	Number of Apples
Sam	🍎🍎🍎🍎🍎
Suzy	🍎🍎🍎🍎🍎🍎🍎
Mike	🍎🍎🍎🍎🍎

18. How many more apples did Suzy collect than Mike?

   (A) 2

   (B) 5

   (C) 6

   (D) 7

19. How many apples did the three friends collect in all?

   (A) 12

   (B) 15

   (C) 17

   (D) 19

20. Jenny had 16 candies. She gave half of her candies to a friend and then ate one of her remaining candies. How many did she have left?

(A) 7

(B) 8

(C) 9

(D) 15

21. Which digit is in the tens place of the number 1,345?

(A) 1

(B) 3

(C) 4

(D) 5

Use the chart below for questions 22 and 23.

Henry asked his classmates which sport was their favorite.

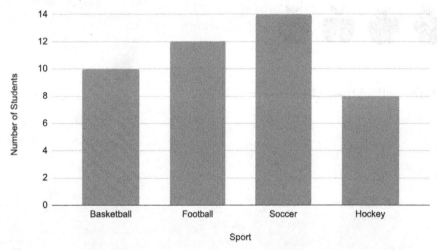

Favorite Sports of 2nd Grade Students

22. Which sport did the most 2nd graders choose as their favorite?

(A) Basketball

(B) Football

(C) Soccer

(D) Hockey

23. How many more students chose basketball than hockey?

    (A) 2

    (B) 3

    (C) 4

    (D) 5

24. Which of the following shows the shape below rotated?

(A)

(B)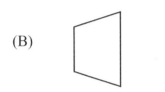

(C)

(D)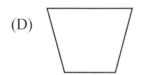

Practice Test #3 Answers

Practice Test #3 - Answers

Auditory Comprehension

1. B	4. B	7. C
2. B	5. C	
3. D	6. A	

Reading Comprehension

1. C	7. B	13. B
2. A	8. A	14. B
3. C	9. C	15. C
4. C	10. D	16. B
5. C	11. B	17. A
6. B	12. D	18. B

Mathematics

1. A	9. C	17. C
2. A	10. D	18. A
3. C	11. A	19. C
4. B	12. C	20. A
5. D	13. B	21. C
6. C	14. B	22. C
7. C	15. B	23. A
8. C	16. C	24. B

Where to Find the Answers

1. **B - The relationship between a lion and his keeper.**

17 went into the cage and led Danco to the uppe.

18 part of it while the repairs were made.

19   William played with the lion for a while,

20 and then both he and Danco fell asleep. The

26 saw the lion and William sleeping side by

27 side contently like two brothers. The

29   The lion woke up and stared at the

30 repairman with an angry look. He placed his

31 paw on William's chest as if to say, "Don't

32 touch him." Then the lion lay down to sleep

37 William, who rubbed his eyes, looked around,

38 and said he was happy with his nap. He shook

39 the lion's paw kindly and then left the cage

40 unharmed.

2. **B - Because he is very strong and looks majestic**

1   The lion is often called the "king of

2 beasts." He is a big and powerful animal,

3 standing three to four feet tall and measuring

4 six to nine feet long. His coat is yellowish-

5 brown, and he has a great, shaggy mane

6 around his neck that makes him look majestic.

7 Lions live in the forests of Asia and Africa,

8 where they are feared by both people and

9 animals. However, if a lion is taken when

3. **D – Danco**

    13 lion named Danco. One day, Danco's cage

4. **B - He thought the lion might hurt him.**

    15 repairman to fix it, but the repairman was too

    16 scared to go near the lion alone. So, William

    23 didn't answer. The repairman got worried that

    24 the lion had hurt William, so he crept around

    33 again. The repairman was worried that

    34 William was hurt. He ran out and told other

5. **C - He led the lion to the upper part of the cage.**

    16 scared to go near the lion alone. So, William

    17 went into the cage and led Danco to the upper

    18 part of it while the repairs were made.

6. **A - comfortably and happily**

    21 repairman finished his work and called out for

    22 William to come and see it, but William

    23 didn't answer. The repairman got worried that

    24 the lion had hurt William, so he crept around

    25 the outside of the cage. To his surprise, he

    26 saw the lion and William sleeping side by

    27 side contently like two brothers. The

7. **C - To prove that the zookeeper was friendly with the lion**

37 William, who rubbed his eyes, looked around,

38 and said he was happy with his nap. He shook

39 the lion's paw kindly and then left the cage

40 unharmed.

Reading Comprehension #3

Where to Find the Answers

Passage 1:

1. **C - The importance of bees and why they are interesting**

   1   Bees are small insects, but they are

   2 very important to our world. Bees help plants

   3 grow by carrying pollen from one flower to

   4 another. This process is called pollination.

   5 Without bees, many plants would not be able

   6 to produce fruits and seeds.

   7   Bees live in large groups called

   8 colonies. Each colony has one queen bee,

   15   Bees make their homes in hives. A

   21   Bees communicate with each other

   22 through a special dance. When a worker bee

   38   Bees are amazing creatures that do a

   39 lot for our environment. It is important to

   40 protect bees so they can continue to help our

   41 plants grow and provide us with honey.

2. **A - One queen bee, many worker bees, and a few drones**

   8 colonies. Each colony has one queen bee,

   9 many worker bees, and a few drones. The

3. C - Find food, build the hive, and take care of young bees

10   queen bee's job is to lay eggs. Worker bees do

11   all the other jobs, like finding food, building

12   the hive, and taking care of the young bees.

4. C – Sections

17   a beekeeper's box. Inside the hive, bees build

18   honeycombs out of wax. The honeycombs

19   have many small cells where bees store honey

20   and pollen and raise their young.

5. C - To communicate where food is located

22   through a special dance. When a worker bee

23   finds a good source of food, it returns to the

24   hive and performs a dance. This dance tells

25   the other bees where the food is located.

6. B - They are fascinating and important to our environment.

38   Bees are amazing creatures that do a

39   lot for our environment. It is important to

Passage 2:

7. B - The steps and tips for planting and taking care of a garden

1   Planting a garden can be a fun and

7   First, you need to choose a good spot

13   Next, decide what you want to plant.

19   Once you have chosen your plants, it

20   is time to start planting. Dig small holes in the

26   After planting, water your garden

27   well. Plants need water to grow, so keep the

31   As your garden grows, you will need

32   to take care of it. Pull out anv weeds that

8. A – An enjoyable way to spend time.

1   Planting a garden can be a fun and

2   rewarding activity. Gardens can be small or

39   Planting a garden can teach you a lot

40   about nature and help you enjoy the outdoors.

41   You will be proud of the beautiful flowers or

42   delicious vegetables you grow. Plus,

43   gardening is a great way to spend time with

44   family and friends. Happy gardening!

9. C – Choose what to plant.

13   Next, decide what you want to plant.

10. D – To give them space to grow

21   soil for your seeds or plants. Make sure to

22   space them out so they have room to grow.

11. B - They can take nutrients and water away from your plants.

32   to take care of it. Pull out any weeds that

33   might grow around your plants. Weeds can

34   take nutrients and water away from your

35   plants. Also, watch out for insects that might

12. D - It is a great way to enjoy nature.

39   Planting a garden can teach you a lot

40 about nature and help you enjoy the outdoors.

41 You will be proud of the beautiful flowers or

42 delicious vegetables you grow. Plus,

43 gardening is a great way to spend time with

44 family and friends. Happy gardening!

Passage 3:

13. B - The life cycle and transformation of a butterfly

35   The life cycle of a butterfly is a

36 wonderful example of nature's magic. From a

37 tiny egg to a beautiful butterfly, the journey is

38 full of changes and surprises. The next time

14. B – Starts eating leaves

9 After a few days, a tiny caterpillar hatches

10 from the egg. The caterpillar is very hungry

11 and starts to eat the leaves around it. As it

15. C – Two weeks

19 body changes completely. This transformation

20 is amazing and takes about two weeks.

16. B - A hard shell around the caterpillar

15   Once the caterpillar is fully grown, it

16 stops eating and finds a safe place to rest. It

17 forms a hard shell around itself called a

18 chrysalis. Inside the chrysalis, the caterpillar's

17. **A - How a caterpillar changes into a butterfly**

35   The life cycle of a butterfly is a

36   wonderful example of nature's magic. From a

37   tiny egg to a beautiful butterfly, the journey is

18. **B - They spread pollen.**

29   Butterflies are not just pretty to look

30   at; they are also important for the

31   environment. As butterflies move from flower

32   to flower, they help plants by spreading

33   pollen. This helps plants grow and produce

34   fruits and seeds.

Mathematics Test 3– How to Solve

1. **A**

Cameron is measuring her cupcake. Approximately, how wide is it?

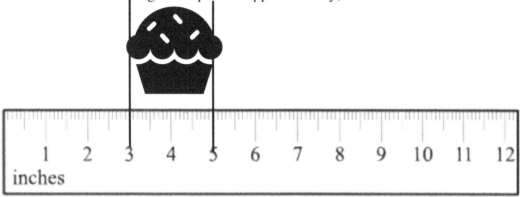

One end of the cupcake is at 3 inches. The other end is at 5 inches.

5 – 3 = 2 inches

2. **A**

Which shows the smallest amount?

(A) $4.34

(B) $4.81

(C) $5.01

(D) $4.90

The smallest one's place value is 4. The smallest tenths place value is 3. So, 4.34 is the smallest.

Use this chart for questions 3 and 4.

Steven counted the number of eggs in his chicken coop each day.

| | Monday | Tuesday | Wednesday | Thursday | Friday |

3. **C**

   On which two days did he see the same number of eggs?

   On Tuesday, he saw 2 eggs. On Thursday, he also saw 2 eggs.

4. **B**

   On which day did he count three eggs in the coop?

   There are three eggs above Wednesday on the chart.

5. **D**

   Stephanie wants to make 3 bracelets for each of her 4 friends. How many bracelets should she make in total?

   $3 + 3 + 3 + 3 = 12$

6. **C**

   Alvin has 24 stuffed animals. He donated 12 stuffed animals. He then got two more for his birthday. How many does he have now?

   24 stuffed animals– 12 donated = 12 stuffed animals

   12 stuffed animals + 2 for his birthday = 14 stuffed animals

142

7. **C**

Which shows an AB pattern?

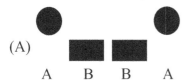

(A)

    A   B   B   A

(B)

    A   B   A   A   B

(C)

    A   B   A   B

(D)

    A   B   A   B   B

8. **C**

Ms. Anita's class collected bags of leaves.

Sam	Mary	Asher	Judah
16.4 oz	15.4 oz	16.8 oz	15.9 oz

All have 1 in the tens place. The highest number in the ones place is 6. So, look just at 16.4 and

16.8. The highest number in the 10ths place is 8, so 16.8 is the highest. Asher collected the most.

9. **C**

What fraction does the shaded part represent?

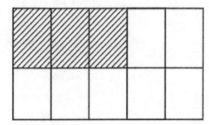

3 shaded out of 10 total

3/10

10. **D**

What is the missing number in the pattern?

3, 6, 12, _?__

In the pattern, each number is doubled.

3 + 3 = 6

6 + 6 = 12

12 + 12 = 24

11. **A**

What number is shown by the shaded squares in the picture?

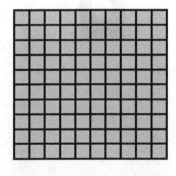 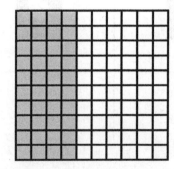 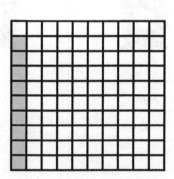

100   +   40   +   9

149

12. **C**

Which of the following shapes is symmetrical across a vertical line?

This means that if you fold it over the line that has been drawn in, both sides will match up. C is the only one that works.

(A)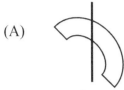

(B)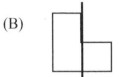

(C)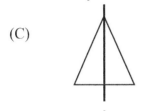

(D)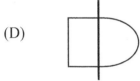

13. **B**

How are these two shapes alike?

They are both rectangles. They are not both squares since the one on the left does not have equal sides. They both have 4 edges, not 6. They are not the same size.

14. **B**

Kayla has 22 stickers. She gave 6 to Sara and 4 to Sally. Which number sentence shows how many she had left?

22 stickers – 6 given to Sara – 4 given to Sally

$22 - 6 - 4 = 12$

15. **B**

Jaelyn has 15 buttons. She wants to split them equally between herself and two other friends. How many should each person get?

She is splitting them into three groups (herself and two friends).

$5 + 5 + 5 = 15$ buttons

5 buttons in each group

16. **C**

Emerson would like to measure flour for cookies. Which is the appropriate unit?

She needs to measure volume for baking. Inches measure length. Pounds measure weight. Cups measure volume. Meters measure length.

17. **C**

Which of the following would have the value of 23 cents?

(A) One quarter and three pennies

   $25 + 3 = 28$

(B) One dime, one nickel, and three pennies

   $10 + 5 + 3 = 18$

(C) Two dimes and three pennies

   $20 + 3 = 23$

(D) Two nickels and three pennies

   $10 + 3 = 13$

Use the chart below for questions 18 and 19.

The chart shows how many apples three friends picked.

Name	Number of Apples
Sam	🍎 🍎 🍎 🍎 🍎
Suzy	🍎 🍎 🍎 🍎 🍎 🍎 🍎
Mike	🍎 🍎 🍎 🍎 🍎

18. **A**

How many more apples did Suzy collect than Mike?

Suzy collected 7 apples. Mike collected 5 apples.

$7 - 5 = 2$ apples

19. **C**

How many apples did the three friends collect in all?

Sam collected 5 apples. Suzy collected 7 apples. Mike collected 5 apples.

$5 + 7 + 5 = 12$

20. **A**

Jenny had 16 candies. She gave half of her candies to a friend and then ate one of her remaining candies. How many did she have left?

Half of 16 is 8.

$16 - 8 = 8$ candies

She then eats one.

$8 - 1 = 7$ candies

21. **C**

Which digit is in the tens place of the number 1,345?

1,3<u>4</u>5

4

Use the chart below for questions 22 and 23.

Henry asked his classmates which sport was their favorite.

22. **C**

Which sport did the most 2nd graders choose as their favorite?

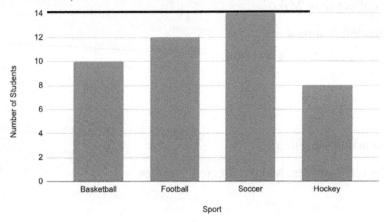

Soccer is the highest bar. 14 students chose soccer.

23. **A**

How many more students chose basketball than hockey?

Favorite Sports of 2nd Grade Students

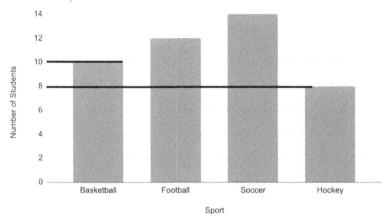

10 students chose basketball. 8 students chose hockey.

$10 - 8 = 2$

24. **B**

Which of the following shows the shape below rotated?

(A)

This shape is wider.

(B)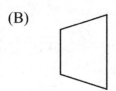

This shape is rotated to the side.

(C)

This shape is taller and thinner.

(D)

This shape is larger.

ISEE
Scoring

How Scoring Works

The ISEE scoring process has a few steps. It starts with your **raw score** which is based on the number of questions you answered correctly. This is then converted into a **scaled score** which is accompanied by a **percentile rank**. This percentile represents how you compare to other test takers. So, if you are in the 89th percentile, this does not mean you answered 89 percent of questions correctly. Instead, it means scored higher than 89 percent of test-takers. Your percentile score is then converted into a **stanine score** with a scale marked from 1 to 9 (9 being the highest.)

You will receive **one** score for auditory/reading comprehension and **one** score for mathematics achievement. The actual scoring is scaled based on the difficulty of the test you receive, so this is just an approximation.

Auditory and Reading Comprehension

Correct Answers (Auditory + Reading)	9	15	19
Percentile	25th	50th	75th

Mathematics

Correct Answers	8	14	18
Percentile	25th	50th	75th

A general rule of thumb to calculate your approximate stanine score is to take your # of correct answers and divide by the total # of questions. The number in the 10s digit of your percentage score is your approximate stanine score. This isn't a perfect rule, but it can be close.

Percentile ——Stanine

1-3 —— 1

4-10——2

11-22——3

23-39——4

40-59——5

60-76——6

77-88——7

89-95——8

96-99——9

Questions or Concerns?

Contact us at larchmontacademics@gmail.com

Made in United States
North Haven, CT
16 November 2024

60399988R00085